MW00934163

ANIMALS:
Guess the Animal Kids Book

65 Real Animal Photos with Interesting Fun Facts

www.selenadale.com

Copyright Notice

THE BONUSES

Get insider info on newly released coloring books, puzzle books, kids books, promotions, freebie alerts and more!

Just to say thank you for purchasing this book, I want to give you 2 free coloring books.

Get Your Free Gifts At The Address Below:

www.selenadale.com/get-your-free-gifts

AT THE END OF THIS BOOK...

CHECK OUT OUR NEW RANGE OF BOOKS INCLUDING:

- MAZE BOOKS

- SUDOKU BOOKS

- WORD SEARCH BOOKS

- COLORING BOOKS FOR ADULTS

- CHILDREN'S ANIMAL BOOKS

...AND MORE!

CONTENTS

7

INTRODUCTION

Welcome to the fun world of guess and learn children's books.

In this book we focus on younger readers who still need that visual content to help them understand what they are reading.

It is targeted at 3 year olds and upwards and is designed to be read with a parent or guardian.

The book has a simple layout so your child can follow along while reading or being read to.

With the guess and learn books you and your child can have fun looking at images of animal silhouettes and guessing what animal it is.

There will be a short list of answers to choose from and on the next page the real animal will be revealed. There will also be some short fun facts to read through for each animal.

We have added as much learning information as possible without making the whole thing seem overwhelming.

As well as learning about animals there is number learning too. At the top of each page we have included the number of the page written in letters and as a number.

This can be read out together with your child which will help them to get to grips with numbers and how they can be written.

Example:
One – 1, Two – 2, Three - 3.

Your child can look at the interesting animal shapes and then guess the name or type of animal it is. Flip over to the next page where the answer is as well as a real photo of that particular animal and a list of fun facts.

This fun preschool children's "learn about animals" book will encourage your child to understand more about the animal kingdom and build their confidence with words and numbers.

The images will help to stimulate your child's imagination and the book can be fun to read anytime, including bedtime...for pre-schoolers and beyond!

<u>ONE - 1</u>

WHAT ANIMAL IS THIS?

- Is it an Ostrich?

- Is it a Cat?

- Is it a Bear?

- Is it a dog?

A BEAR

FUN FACTS:

- Bears have two layers of fur. A short layer to keep the bear warm and a long layer to keep water away from its skin.

- Bears live as long as 30 years in the wild.

- Bears are bowlegged. This gives them better grip and balance.

WHAT ANIMAL IS THIS?

- Is it a Dog?
- Is it a Cat?
- Is it a Rhinoceros?
- Is it an elephant?

A CAT

FUN FACTS:

- Cats sleep for an average of 13 to 15 hours a day.

- Cats have powerful night vision and can see 6 times better than humans in the dark.

- Generally, cats live for around 12 to 15 years.

THREE - 3

WHAT ANIMAL IS THIS?

- Is it a Crab?
- Is it a Tiger?
- Is it a Frog?
- Is it a Fish?

A CRAB

FUN FACTS:

- Crabs use their gills to help them breathe. That is why they need to stay close to the water.

- Just like snails, Crabs have eyes on their stalks, but they see a lot less detail than human eyes.

- Crabs eat algae, fungi, bacteria and worms.

FOUR - 4

WHAT ANIMAL IS THIS?

- Is it a Dolphin?

- Is it a Monkey?

- Is it a Duck?

- Is it a Rat?

A DUCK

FUN FACTS:

- A baby duck is called a duckling, an adult male is a drake and an adult female duck is called a hen.

- Ducks have waterproof feathers. It can dive underwater and stay completely dry.

- Ducks eat grass, plants, insects, seeds, fruit and fish.

FIVE - 5

WHAT ANIMAL IS THIS?

- Is it an Elephant?

- Is it a Kangaroo?

- Is it a Goat?

- Is it a Horse?

AN ELEPHANT

FUN FACTS:

- Elephants are the largest land-living mammal in the world.

- An adult elephant needs to drink around 210 litres of water a day.

- An elephant will use its trunk to put food into its mouth and suck up water to drink.

SIX - 6

WHAT ANIMAL IS THIS?

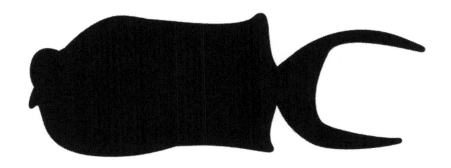

- Is it a Dolphin?
- Is it a Frog?
- Is it a Fish?
- Is it an Anteater?

A GOLDFISH

FUN FACTS:

- Goldfish have to sleep with their eyes open because they have no eyelids.

- Goldfish can live up to 30 years.

- Goldfish have teeth in their throat which are used to help them crush their food.

SEVEN - 7

WHAT ANIMAL IS THIS?

- Is it a Penguin?
- Is it a Frog?
- Is it a Shark?
- Is it an Eagle?

A FROG

FUN FACTS:

- Frogs are amphibians which means they can live both on land and in water.

- Frogs don't drink water, they soak it into their body through their skin.

- Frogs can see forwards, sideways and upwards all at the same time.

EIGHT - 8

WHAT ANIMAL IS THIS?

- Is it a Giraffe?

- Is it a Monkey?

- Is it a Snake?

- Is it a Cat?

A GIRAFFE

FUN FACTS:

- Giraffes have spots that cover their fur. The spots act as a camouflage to protect from predators.

- Giraffes have four stomachs which help digest tough food.

- Giraffes have tough, bluish-purple tongues that are covered in bristly hair. This helps them when eating thorny trees.

<u>NINE - 9</u>

WHAT ANIMAL IS THIS?

- Is it a Kangaroo?

- Is it a Cat?

- Is it a Snake?

- Is it a Bear?

A KANGAROO

FUN FACTS:

- Kangaroos can hop around on two legs or walk around on its legs and arms.

- They eat grass, flowers, leaves, ferns, moss and even insects.

- Kangaroos have excellent hearing and are able to move their ears in different directions without moving their head.

WHAT ANIMAL IS THIS?

- Is it an Anteater?

- Is it a Snake?

- Is it a Lion?

- Is it a Scorpion?

A LION

FUN FACTS:

- Lions can run very fast, up to 81kph but they get tired quickly.

- The roar of a lion is loud and can be heard from 8 kilometers away.

- Lions rest for up to 20 hours a day and live for around 12 years.

<u>ELEVEN - 11</u>

WHAT ANIMAL IS THIS?

- Is it a Seal?

- Is it a Horse?

- Is it a Monkey?

- Is it a Camel?

A MONKEY

FUN FACTS:

- Monkeys communicate by using vocalizations, facial expressions, and body movements.

- They live in trees, grasslands, mountains, forests and on high plains.

- Most monkeys eat both animals and plants.

- Monkeys can use their fingers and their toes to grab things.

WHAT ANIMAL IS THIS?

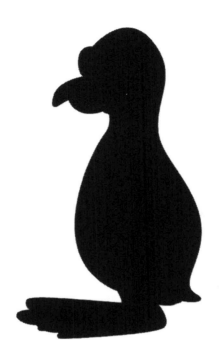

- Is it a Penguin?

- Is it a Sheep?

- Is it a Lion?

- Is it a Spider?

A PENGUIN

FUN FACTS:

- Penguins slide on their tummies over ice and snow so they can travel fast and have fun!

- Penguins find all their food in the sea and eat fish, squid, crabs and shrimp.

- Penguins swallow pebbles and stones to help digest their food.

THIRTEEN - 13

WHAT ANIMAL IS THIS?

- Is it a Frog?

- Is it a Wolf?

- Is it a Rabbit?

- Is it a Cow?

A RABBIT

FUN FACTS:

- Rabbits are born with their eyes closed and without fur and live for around 10 years.

- Rabbits stand upright on their hind legs to look for predators.

- Rabbits love to dig so if you have a pet rabbit make sure you keep some sand or earth in its hutch.

FOURTEEN - 14

WHAT ANIMAL IS THIS?

- Is it a Giraffe?
- Is it a Rhinoceros?
- Is it a Raccoon?
- Is it a Moose?

37

A RHINOCEROS

FUN FACTS:

- Rhinoceroses have very thick skin to protect them from harm but it is also quite sensitive to sunburn and insect bites.

- Rhinos look like they are slow, but can actually run up to 40 mph / 64kph.

- Rhinos need to drink once a day and so they make sure they stay within 5km of water.

FIFTEEN - 15

WHAT ANIMAL IS THIS?

- Is it a Shark?
- Is it a Cat?
- Is it a Penguin?
- Is it a Mouse?

A SHARK

FUN FACTS:

- Three of the most dangerous sharks are the Great White Shark, the Hammerhead Shark and the Tiger Shark.

- Sharks never run out of teeth. They have rows of backup teeth that spin forward to replace any lost teeth. A shark may lose up to 20,000 teeth in its lifetime!

- If a shark stops moving then it will suffocate and die. So it needs to keep moving to deliver oxygen to the blood stream.

WHAT ANIMAL IS THIS?

- Is it a Zebra?

- Is it a Frog?

- Is it a Vulture?

- Is it a Lizard?

A VULTURE

FUN FACTS:

- Vultures prefer to eat fresh meat but are able to consume rotten dead animal carcasses.

- Vultures have excellent senses of sight and smell. They can find a dead animal from a mile or more away.

- Vultures have a very powerful digestive system that contains special acids that dissolve the meat it swallows.

WHAT ANIMAL IS THIS?

- Is it a Panda Bear?

- Is it a Mouse?

- Is it a Whale?

- Is it a Dog?

A WHALE

FUN FACTS:

- Whales communicate by singing. Sometimes they sing to call a friend or just to have fun.

- Whales are mammals, which means they need to come up for air, unlike fish which can breathe underwater.

- Whales must rise to the surface often to breathe. So, to stay alive, only half of their brain sleeps if they ever feel tired.

EIGHTEEN - 18

WHAT ANIMAL IS THIS?

- Is it a Penguin?

- Is it an Anteater?

- Is it a Deer?

- Is it a Dog?

AN ANTEATER

FUN FACTS:

- Anteaters don't have any teeth. They use their long and sticky tongue to catch prey.

- Anteaters have poor eyesight, but have an excellent sense of smell. They use their nose to find food.

- They sleep 15 hours per day and live up to 15 years in the wild.

- The giant anteater can eat 30,000 insects a day.

WHAT ANIMAL IS THIS?

- Is it a Buffalo?

- Is it a Tiger?

- Is it a Frog?

- Is it a Crocodile?

A BUFFALO

FUN FACTS:

- Buffaloes are good swimmers and often cross deep water in search of better sources of food.

- The hide on a bull buffalo's neck is as thick as 2 inches.

- Water buffaloes use their horns to protect against predators such as, tigers, lions and crocodiles.

- The water buffalo is a plant-eater and eats plants, grass, leaves and herbs.

TWENTY- 20

WHAT ANIMAL IS THIS?

- Is it a Dolphin?

- Is it a Camel?

- Is it a Whale?

- Is it a Duck?

A CAMEL

FUN FACTS:

- A camel's hump does not store water, it stores fat.

- Camels have two rows of thick eyelashes to protect their eyes from the desert dust.

- Camels can drink up to seven litres of water a day. They can survive without water for up to two months.

WHAT ANIMAL IS THIS?

- Is it a Crocodile?
- Is it a Kangaroo?
- Is it a Goat?
- Is it a Snake?

A CROCODILE

FUN FACTS:

- Crocodiles have sharp teeth and have the strongest bite of any animal in the world.

- Crocodiles eat a variety of meats including fish, birds and other animals. Crocs can survive for a long time without food.

- Crocs don't chew their food. They tear apart flesh and swallow large chunks of meat.

- Crocodiles have excellent eyesight and see really well at night.

WHAT ANIMAL IS THIS?

- Is it a Dolphin?

- Is it a Mole?

- Is it a Whale?

- Is it a Deer?

A DEER

FUN FACTS:

- Deers can turn their ears in any direction without moving their head. They have a great sense of hearing.

- Deer have their eyes on the sides of their head, giving them a 310 degree view.

- They have powerful leg muscles and can run 40mph and jump 10 feet high.

- Deers eat grass, leaves, stems, shoots, berries, herbs, acorns, mushrooms and fruit

WHAT ANIMAL IS THIS?

- Is it a Dolphin?
- Is it a Tiger?
- Is it a Shark?
- Is it a Goldfish?

A DOLPHIN

FUN FACTS:

- Dolphins need air to survive. When they sleep they rest one side of the brain at a time so they can continue to rise to the surface for air.

- Dolphins use a blowhole on top of their heads to breathe.

- They can jump up to 20 feet out of the water.

- Dolphins are very social animals and communicate by clicking, whistling to each other.

WHAT ANIMAL IS THIS?

- Is it a Hamster?

- Is it a Giraffe?

- Is it a Snake?

- Is it a Penguin?

A HAMSTER

FUN FACTS:

- Hamsters are short sighted and color blind.

- They eat fresh vegetables, berries, seeds, nuts and meat. Wild hamsters eat insects too.

- Hamsters are more active at night and they sleep during the day.

- They can store their food in their cheeks and then take it to their home to eat it all later.

WHAT ANIMAL IS THIS?

- Is it a Kangaroo?
- Is it a Hedgehog?
- Is it a Snake?
- Is it a Rhino?

A HEDGEHOG

FUN FACTS:

- Hedgehogs sleep all day and come out at night.

- They have thick, spiny coats to help protect them against predators such as the fox.

- Hedgehogs have about 5000 spines. Each spine lasts about a year then drops out. New spines then grow back.

- They use their long, extending snout to help them sniff out food.

WHAT ANIMAL IS THIS?

- Is it an Anteater?

- Is it a Hippopotamus?

- Is it a Lion?

- Is it a Camel?

HIPPOPOTAMUSES

FUN FACTS:

- Hippopotamuses love to spend time in water such as rivers, lakes and swamps.

- Hippos typically live for about 45 years and mostly eat grass.

- Hippos can swim quite well and can hold their breath for up to five minutes.

- These big animals can be aggressive and are considered a dangerous animal in Africa.

TWENTY-SEVEN – 27

WHAT ANIMAL IS THIS?

- Is it a Seal?

- Is it a Horse?

- Is it a Cat?

- Is it an Eel?

A HORSE

FUN FACTS:

- Horses have a lifespan of around 25 years and can sleep both lying down and standing up.

- Horses mostly eat hay and grass. They also like peas, beans, fruit and sweet vegetables like carrots.

- Horses have amazing senses of sound, sight and smell and a tremendous sense of balance.

WHAT ANIMAL IS THIS?

- Is it a Penguin?
- Is it a Sheep?
- Is it a Frog?
- Is it a Hyena?

A HYENA

FUN FACTS:

- Hyenas are known to scavenge food from other animals such as Lions.

- When they hunt they chase down animals such as wildebeests, gazelles and zebras.

- Hyenas can see really well in the dark.

- They don't need to drink a lot of water to survive.

- Hyenas generally live no more than 20 years in the wild.

WHAT ANIMAL IS THIS?

- Is it a Jellyfish?

- Is it a Wolf?

- Is it a Shark?

- Is it a Rabbit?

A JELLYFISH

FUN FACTS:

- Jellyfish live in the sea and are found in all oceans but some live in fresh water too.

- Jellyfish use their tentacles to sting. Getting stung can be very painful.

- These strange creatures don't have any bones, hearts or brains.

- Jellyfish mainly eat tiny fish, fish eggs and other jellyfish.

WHAT ANIMAL IS THIS?

- Is it a Giraffe?

- Is it a Rhinoceros?

- Is it a Vulture?

- Is it a Lizard?

A LIZARD

FUN FACTS:

- Lizards smell by licking in the air just like snakes do.

- There are many types of lizards. Their sizes range from a few centimeters to a few meters.

- Small lizards such as Geckos eat crickets, spiders, insects, cockroaches, grasshoppers, beetles and ants.

- The Komodo Dragon is one of the largest lizards and is very dangerous.

WHAT ANIMAL IS THIS?

- Is it a Shark?

- Is it a Panda?

- Is it a Penguin?

- Is it a Duck?

71

A PANDA

FUN FACTS:

- Giant pandas live in China and have a black and white coat with large black patches around their eyes.

- Pandas live for around 20 years in the wild and they mostly eat bamboo. They will sometimes eat leaves, stalks and berries.

- A giant panda's fur is quite thick and wiry and can grow up to 4 inches.

- Pandas have a tough special lining in their throat to protect it from bamboo splinters.

WHAT ANIMAL IS THIS?

- Is it a Zebra?

- Is it a Panda?

- Is it a Kangaroo?

- Is it a Peacock?

A PEACOCK

FUN FACTS:

- Peacocks are one of the largest flying birds and their length can reach 5 feet.

- They like to eat insects, frogs, toads, berries, figs, leaves, flowers and seeds.

- The male peacock attracts a female by showing off his beautiful colored feathers.

- When a male peacock gets angry he will fan his tail out in order to make himself look bigger.

THIRTY-THREE - 33

WHAT ANIMAL IS THIS?

- Is it a Panda Bear?
- Is it a Mouse?
- Is it a Hyena?
- Is it a Pelican?

A PELICAN

FUN FACTS:

- Pelicans are huge birds that have a wingspan of 5 meters and are able to fly really high up in the sky.

- They like to eat fish, tadpoles and sometimes even turtles.

- A Pelican's beak can hold 3 buckets of fish in one scoop.

WHAT ANIMAL IS THIS?

- Is it a Penguin?
- Is it an Anteater?
- Is it a Lion?
- Is it a Pig?

A PIG

FUN FACTS:

- Pigs eat both plants and other animals.

- Pigs are intelligent, peaceful animals that have a tremendous sense of smell.

- They are social animals and like to snuggle close to one another while sleeping nose to nose.

- Pigs have short legs and look fat but they can run up to 11mph.

WHAT ANIMAL IS THIS?

- Is it a Rabbit?
- Is it a Mouse?
- Is it a Jellyfish?
- Is it a Raccoon?

RACCOONS

FUN FACTS:

- Raccoons eat plants and animals such as fruits, nuts, acorns, insects, frogs, fish, and bird eggs.

- Raccoons that live in urban areas have learned to eat trash and other food out of trash cans.

- Raccoons mostly come out at night. They hide from coyotes, wolves, hawks and owls who will try to eat them.

WHAT ANIMAL IS THIS?

- Is it a Buffalo?

- Is it a Tiger?

- Is it a Seahorse?

- Is it a Goldfish?

A SEAHORSE

FUN FACTS:

- Seahorses like to swim in pairs with their tails linked together.

- These pretty creatures move around in the water by using a small fin on their back that flutters really fast.

- Seahorses have to eat all the time because they do not have a stomach. The food just passes through their bodies.

WHAT ANIMAL IS THIS?

- Is it a Seagull?

- Is it a Camel?

- Is it a Duck?

- Is it a Raccoon?

A SEAGULL

FUN FACTS:

- Seagulls are very intelligent birds. They learn quickly and have good memories.

- Seagulls have special glands which flush salt from their systems which means they can drink salt water if they need to.

- These birds eat insects, earthworms, small rodents, reptiles, seed, fruit and trash left by humans.

WHAT ANIMAL IS THIS?

- Is it a Crocodile?
- Is it a Kangaroo?
- Is it an Anteater?
- Is it a Sloth?

SLOTHS

FUN FACTS:

- Sloths have toes that look like big hooked claws. These claws are their only defence against predators.

- Their main predators are Jaguars, snakes and Eagles.

- Sloths sleep for 10 hours a day and can live up to 40 years.

  Sloths are very slow, they only move 13 feet a minute.

WHAT ANIMAL IS THIS?

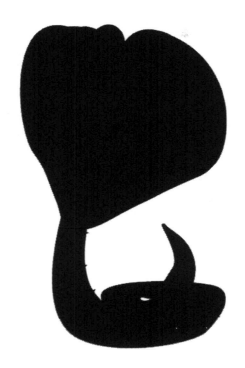

- Is it a Snake?

- Is it a Lion?

- Is it a Deer?

- Is it a Crocodile?

A SNAKE

FUN FACTS:

- Snakes have flexible jaws which allow them to eat bigger animals. Snakes can't bite so they have to swallow animals whole.

- Snake fangs are very sharp. When they bite, venom is released to kill or paralyze its prey. Some snakes do not have venom.

- Snakes are meat eaters. They eat insects, rodents, birds, eggs, fish, frogs, lizards and other small animals.

FOURTY - 40

WHAT ANIMAL IS THIS?

- Is it a Dolphin?
- Is it a Tiger?
- Is it a Shark?
- Is it a Crab?

A TIGER

FUN FACTS:

- Tigers look slow but they can run up to 40 mph and can jump 5 metres in length.

- Tiger cubs leave their mother when they are around 2 years of age.

- These big cats are meat eaters and eat deer, frogs, monkeys, porcupines, wild boar and even lizards.

- When it gets too hot, Tigers will cool off in lakes and streams.

FOURTY-ONE - 41

WHAT ANIMAL IS THIS?

- Is it a Hamster?

- Is it a Giraffe?

- Is it a Mouse?

- Is it a Zebra?

A ZEBRA

FUN FACTS:

- Zebras have excellent eyesight and hearing.

- They sleep standing up.

- They are fast runners and have excellent stamina. They can run up to 65kph.

- Zebras eat mostly grasses but sometimes they will eat shrubs, herbs, twigs and leaves.

WHAT ANIMAL IS THIS?

- Is it a Sheep?

- Is it an Anteater?

- Is it an Elephant?

- Is it a Bat?

A BAT

FUN FACTS:

- There are over 1000 different types of Bat in the world.

- Most Bats feed on insects and can consume up to 6,000 insects each night!

- Some Bats also eat fruit, fish or even blood!

- Bats live for many years. They live between 10 and 30 years.

- Bats see in the dark by using a special skill that involves sound waves and echoes.

FOURTY-THREE - 43

WHAT ANIMAL IS THIS?

- Is it a Cow?
- Is it a Beaver?
- Is it a Horse?
- Is it a Cheetah?

A BEAVER

FUN FACTS:

- Beavers are very good swimmers and live in streams and lakes with trees.

- Beavers have see-through eyelids which helps them to see under water.

- Their homes are made out of branches and mud and are called Lodges.

- Beavers use their stiff tails to steer under water and for balance while they wonder around on land.

FOURTY-FOUR - 44

WHAT ANIMAL IS THIS?

- Is it a Cheetah?
- Is it a Tiger?
- Is it a Frog?
- Is it a Pelican?

A CHEETAH

FUN FACTS:

- The cheetah is the fastest land animal in the world. Their top speeds can reach up to 70mph.

- Cheetahs cannot roar, but they do purr very loudly...just like your cat at home!

- Cheetahs hunt for food during the day because they have bad night vision.

- To survive, they only need to drink once every three to four days.

FOURTY-FIVE - 45

WHAT ANIMAL IS THIS?

- Is it a Dolphin?
- Is it a Camel?
- Is it a Pig?
- Is it a Chicken?

A CHICKEN

FUN FACTS:

- Chickens eat worms, insects, seeds, grains, snails, slugs, fruits and vegetables.

- Chicken Hens can lay up to 300 eggs per year.

- They cannot fly very high but can get airborne enough to make it over a fence.

- Chickens take "dust baths". They roll around in the dirt to clean themselves from any parasites.

WHAT ANIMAL IS THIS?

- Is it a Crocodile?

- Is it a Kangaroo?

- Is it a Snail?

- Is it a Cow?

A COW

FUN FACTS:

- Cows do not eat meat. They eat grasses, plants and corn.

- They can live up to 25 years.

- A cow can produce 6 gallons of milk a day! With Cow's milk we can make butter, cream, ice cream and cheese.

- Cows have 4 stomachs to help digest their food properly.

FOURTY-SEVEN - 47

WHAT ANIMAL IS THIS?

- Is it a Dog?
- Is it a Rat?
- Is it a Lion?
- Is it a Panda?

A DOG

FUN FACTS:

- Dogs have amazing hearing senses and can hear sounds at least four times the distance that humans can.

- On average a dog can live up to 14 years of age.

- The Greyhound is the fastest dog on Earth and can reach speeds of up to 45mph.

- A dog's whiskers are so sensitive that they can detect small changes in the air.

FOURTY-EIGHT - 48

WHAT ANIMAL IS THIS?

- Is it a Flamingo?

- Is it a Cat?

- Is it an Octopus?

- Is it a Hedgehog?

A FLAMINGO

FUN FACTS:

- Flamingos hold their bills upside down while skimming the water so they can filter out their food.

- A Flamingo's legs are longer than their entire body and can be 30-50 inches long.

- Wild Flamingoes live for around 20-30 years.

- Flamingos conserve their energy by resting and sleeping on one leg.

- Their webbed feet help them to swim and move around in soft mud.

FOURTY-NINE - 49

WHAT ANIMAL IS THIS?

- Is it a Hamster?

- Is it a Giraffe?

- Is it a Monkey?

- Is it a Goat?

A GOAT

FUN FACTS:

- Goats have excellent balance and coordination which means some can survive high up in the mountains.

- Baby goats are called "Kids". They stand up and walk within minutes of being born.

- Goats are very good climbers and can climb to the tops of trees if they want to.

- Goats eat hay, bushes, fresh grass, grains and nibble on almost anything.

FIFTY - 50

WHAT ANIMAL IS THIS?

- Is it a Kangaroo?

- Is it a Hedgehog?

- Is it a Butterfly?

- Is it a Gorilla?

A GORILLA

FUN FACTS:

- Gorillas mainly eat leaves, shoots, stems and fruit. Sometimes they eat small animals such as grubs, caterpillars, snails, termites and ants.

- Gorillas spend a lot of their time on the ground rather than in the trees.

- A gorilla can live in the wild for up to 50 years.

- Gorillas are very smart animals.

FIFTY-ONE - 51

WHAT ANIMAL IS THIS?

- Is it an Anteater?

- Is it a Hippopotamus?

- Is it a Peacock?

- Is it a Koala?

A KOALA

FUN FACTS:

- Koalas spend most of their lives asleep in trees. They sleep for up to 18 hours.

- Koalas get most of their moisture from leaves so they do not drink much water.

- A baby koala spends its first six months in its mother's pouch.

- Koalas climb trees using their sharp claws.

WHAT ANIMAL IS THIS?

- Is it a Moose?

- Is it a Horse?

- Is it a Tiger?

- Is it a Seagull?

A MOOSE

FUN FACTS:

- A male Moose sheds its antlers in the winter and grows them back in the spring.

- Wild Moose live for an average of 25 years.

- Moose have hooves that are perfect for walking through snowy, muddy and marshy ground.

- Moose are excellent swimmers and can swim up to 6mph.

- A moose can run non-stop for up to 15 miles and at speeds of up to 35mph.

WHAT ANIMAL IS THIS?

- Is it a Penguin?

- Is it a Sheep?

- Is it a Hippo?

- Is it an Octopus?

AN OCTOPUS

FUN FACTS:

- All octopuses are venomous. The most dangerous of these are the blue-ringed octopuses.

- Octopuses have four pairs of arms which adds up to eight altogether.

- Octopuses have three hearts.

- They have a beak which looks like a parrot beak.

WHAT ANIMAL IS THIS?

- Is it an Owl?

- Is it a Wolf?

- Is it a Hamster?

- Is it a Jellyfish?

AN OWL

FUN FACTS:

- Owls can see things at a distance very well but they can't see things close to their eyes clearly.

- Owls have 3 eyelids. One is for blinking, one for sleeping and one for keeping the eye clean.

- Owls don't just hoot; they can make all kinds of sounds such as screeches, whistles, barks and hisses.

WHAT ANIMAL IS THIS?

- Is it a Giraffe?

- Is it a Polar Bear?

- Is it a Tiger?

- Is it a Lizard?

A POLAR BEAR

FUN FACTS:

- Polar bears are able to stay dry due to their water repellent fur.

- Polar bears do not slip on the ice because they have rough surfaces on their paws.

- Their fur is so thick that sometimes they get too hot rather than too cold.

- Polar bears are great swimmers and can reach speeds of 6mph in the water.

WHAT ANIMAL IS THIS?

- Is it a Shark?

- Is it a Panda?

- Is it a Squirrel?

- Is it a Rat?

A RAT

FUN FACTS:

- Rats are social animals and need companions. If they are on their own they get very sad and lonely.

- Rats are very clean animals and spend a lot of time grooming themselves.

- Just like a camel, a rat can go without having a drink of water for a long time.

- Rats are very smart animals and have excellent memories.

FIFTY-SEVEN - 57

WHAT ANIMAL IS THIS?

- Is it a Zebra?

- Is it a Panda?

- Is it a Skunk?

- Is it a Scorpion?

A SCORPION

FUN FACTS:

- Baby Scorpions ride on their mother's back until they grow big enough to crawl around on their own.

- All Scorpions are venomous but not all are deadly. About 25 Scorpions have dangerous venom.

- Scorpions are meat eaters and usually feed on insects.

- Scorpions prefer to come out at night.

FIFTY-EIGHT - 58

WHAT ANIMAL IS THIS?

- Is it a Sheep?

- Is it a Mouse?

- Is it a Cheetah?

- Is it a Pelican?

SHEEP

FUN FACTS:

- Sheep have a 300 degree field of vision which means they can see behind without having to turn their head.

- They are smart animals and have very good memories.

- A Sheep's thick wool protects it from the heat and cold.

- Sheep's milk is perfect for making cheese.

FIFTY-NINE - 59

WHAT ANIMAL IS THIS?

- Is it a Penguin?

- Is it an Anteater?

- Is it a Stingray?

- Is it a Skunk?

A SKUNK

FUN FACTS:

- Skunks eat plants and animals. They eat fruits, insects, worms, reptiles and rodents.

- When threatened, a Skunk will spray an oily and smelly liquid from under its tail.

- They have a good sense of smell and hearing but bad eyesight.

- Skunks love to eat honeybees.

SIXTY - 60

WHAT ANIMAL IS THIS?

- Is it a Squirrel?
- Is it a Tiger?
- Is it a Giraffe?
- Is it a Seahorse?

A SQUIRREL

FUN FACTS:

- Squirrels prepare for the winter months by burying their food. This keeps the food stored away for when it gets cold.

- When a squirrel is scared it will either keep still or climb up a tree to safety.

- Squirrels are very smart animals.

- There are also flying squirrels that can glide in the air between trees.

WHAT ANIMAL IS THIS?

- Is it a Stingray?

- Is it a Camel?

- Is it a Rabbit?

- Is it a Duck?

A STINGRAY

FUN FACTS:

- Stingrays have a flattened body with a long tail that usually contains venom.

- Stingrays hide on the ocean floor covered under the sand so enemies cannot see them.

- They eat small sea animals such as oysters, crabs, snails and some fish.

- Stingrays like to live in shallow waters and warm climates.

- There are at least 70 different types of Stingray in the world.

WHAT ANIMAL IS THIS?

- Is it a Crocodile?

- Is it a Kangaroo?

- Is it a Beaver?

- Is it a Swan?

A SWAN

FUN FACTS:

- Swans are pretty fast and can fly at speeds of up to 60mph.

- Swans are highly intelligent and have great memories.

- They protect themselves by hissing, pecking or flapping their wings.

- Swans like to eat underwater plants, stems, leaves and roots. They also eat any insects.

WHAT ANIMAL IS THIS?

- Is it a Snake?

- Is it a Lion?

- Is it a Penguin?

- Is it a Tortoise?

A TORTOISE

FUN FACTS:

- Tortoises have good eyesight and an excellent sense of smell.

- Tortoises can live for a very long time; similar to humans. Some can live up to 100 years or older.

- They mainly eat grass, ferns, fruits, flowers and tree leaves.

- Tortoises hibernate during winter months.

WHAT ANIMAL IS THIS?

- Is it a Turkey?
- Is it a Crocodile?
- Is it a Bear?
- Is it a Shark?

A TURKEY

FUN FACTS:

- Turkeys are sensitive animals that are highly social and pretty smart too.

- Wild turkeys can fly at up to 55 mph for a short distance.

- Turkeys can run at speeds of up to 25mph.

- The long fleshy object that hangs over their beak is called a snood.

WHAT ANIMAL IS THIS?

- Is it a Hamster?

- Is it a Wolf?

- Is it a Snail?

- Is it a Spider?

A WOLF

FUN FACTS:

- Wolves are good swimmers and can swim distances of up to 8 miles.

- A Wolf can run up to 40 mph if it has to.

- Wolves are excellent hunters and hunt in groups called a pack.

- If a Wolf hunts alone it will catch small animals such as squirrels, hares, chipmunks, raccoons or rabbits. They live up to 30 years in the wild.

MORE FUN BOOKS HERE!

Check them out on the next pages!

All book collections can be found on

www.selenadale.com

Or find all collections on Amazon:

- amazon.com/author/selenadale
- amazon.com/author/puzzleplanet
- amazon.com/author/childrenslearning
- amazon.com/author/coloring-books-wonderland

CHILDREN'S EARLY LEARNING BOOKS

 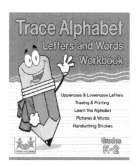

Go To:

selenadale.com

amazon.com/author/childrenslearning

FUN ANIMAL LEARNING BOOKS

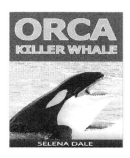  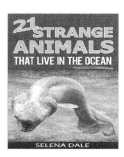

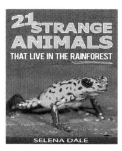  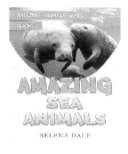

Go To:

selenadale.com

amazon.com/author/selenadale

PUZZLE BOOKS FOR ADULTS

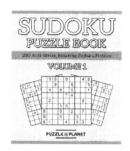  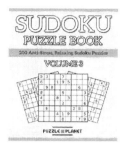

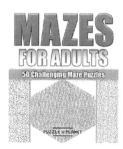  

Go To:

selenadale.com

amazon.com/author/puzzleplanet

WORD SEARCH BOOKS COLLECTION

Go To:

selenadale.com

amazon.com/author/puzzleplanet

COLORING BOOKS FOR ADULTS

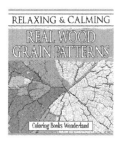  

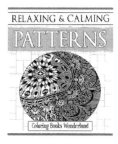  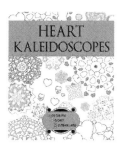

Go To:

selenadale.com

amazon.com/author/coloring-books-wonderland

NEW CHILDREN'S ANIMAL ADVENTURE BOOKS THAT MIX IN REAL LIFE ANIMAL FACTS

Go To:

selenadale.com

amazon.com/author/selenadale

Made in the USA
San Bernardino, CA
12 February 2017